D1512652

THE SUN IS OPEN

Gail McConnell is from Belfast. She is the author of two poetry pamphlets: *Fothermather* (Ink Sweat & Tears, 2019) and *Fourteen* (Green Bottle Press, 2018). *Fothermather* was shortlisted for the Michael Marks Poetry Award and made into a programme for Radio 4 and the *Seriously...* podcast, produced by Conor Garrett. Gail's poems have appeared in *The Poetry Review, PN Review, Virginia Quarterly Review, Blackbox Manifold* and *Stand,* and she is the recipient of two awards from the Arts Council of Northern Ireland. She is Senior Lecturer in English at Queen's University Belfast and the author of *Northern Irish Poetry and Theology* (Palgrave, 2014). Gail's writing interests include violence, creatureliness, queerness and the possibilities and politics of language and form.

ALSO BY GAIL McCONNELL

POETRY

Fothermather (Ink Sweat & Tears, 2019)
Fourteen (Green Bottle Press, 2018)

CRITICISM

Northern Irish Poetry and Theology (Palgrave, 2014)

The Sun is Open

GAIL McCONNELL

Penned in the Margins
LONDON

PUBLISHED BY PENNED IN THE MARGINS
Toynbee Studios, 28 Commercial Street, London E1 6AB
www.pennedinthemargins.co.uk

First published 2021

Printed in the United Kingdom by TJ Books Ltd

ISBN
978-1-908058-92-8

Grey text denotes material found from
sources listed in the notes on p.119

THE SUN IS OPEN

ON THE MORNING of March 6, 1984, Mr. William McConnell, assistant governor of the Maze Prison, was outside his home, checking underneath his car for explosive devices, when he was shot dead in front of his wife and three-year-old daughter.

BEGIN WITH VICTIM on his
back is how this could begin
place your mouth over his mouth
pinch his nostrils shut easier to
take what I have found and break
it up breathe steadily till victim's
chest begins to rise pause
every minute to glue it back
the wrong way take a deep breath
yourself if there is no air
exchange do not touch him

YOU COME into this world
head first come in on your rump
they call it breech you may be
lifted   out

I'm   making   soft   returns
for this you need two keys SHIFT
and ENTER to go down the line
carries on the carriage moving
back

our house was on a street that
slanted at the bottom a
carriageway you didn't cross
four lanes all going fifty to
a roundabout nearby the dog
next door was Honey
a lab as old as me who loved
to lie on the just
cut lawn and sniff her tail
going in the afternoon sun

I played a game with
ladders and a bird inside a cage
on my BBC you typed in rows
and rows of code it made no
sense they were commands the
screen was black without but
when you'd hit the last RETURN
a snake curved round & round
& round until you turned it

my teeth are made of milk
deciduous he calls them
mum goes first three sound two
sound one sound one two three
the nurse writes it all down she
rinses then it's me I see the hairs
inside his nose my mouth all big
he taps each tooth E D C B A A B
C D E only there's a gap where C
should be before you hit the sack
get rid of plaque says SuperTed
a spotty man from outer space
brought him to life with cosmic
dust I stick it on the wall fight
tooth decay the He-Man way
when I wake up it's gone under
my pillow

there's a coin

she's still asleep I watch cartoons
Bananaman smiles back at me
then Doctor Gloom whacks him
with a mallet BONK his head's
submerged inside his chest his
eyes roll round and round the
doctor points the gun directs the
age-reversing rays and turns him
to a baby with one tooth the crow
has a banana and what saves the
day's a mirror purple rays
bounce back now the doctor's
just a tot

there was a time when I was Brian like our neighbour six doors down I had a skateboard with a monkey skull on the underside my cards read Happy Birthday Brian whose dad we knew not to say was in the police that day he must have been dead scared hearing the shots they're coming now for him for me he might have thought he had a test in school that day he knew if x then y but couldn't make the pencil cross the page it lay along his pointer then he folded back three fingers raised his thumb to make a gun shape

God made the sun the stars
the moon or did he make the
bang we learned about the Milky
Way not just a chocolate bar
with soft white air inside it is a
spiral whirlpool of stars and one
out there on the edge is yellow
that's our sun

night and day he made and trees
and peas and wendy houses
tricycles sunglasses that go snap
let there be light let lights appear
and let the air be filled with birds
the little hinge that moves
their legs like knees my elbows
knees and toes all numbered
are the very hairs of my head
and even all my bones

dream about a man in a car
engine his head sticking out the
car ramming into doors him
going into them head first when
he stands up there's no top on
his head you can see inside
coils of uncooked sausages in
there he pirouettes falls to the
ground   raw   meat   where
the mind should be or what it is
plump white skin so pale

screw worm comes in through
the wounds some have no head
have an eye instead a screw eye
lets a loop occur lift up the
loupe   &   look

dirt underneath my nails I see it
through   the   white   outside
the dining room a square of tiles
the   sunlight   never
reaches   slaters   under   scatter
as I pry one up scurry to the
corners   disappear

you assemble it yourself it
came flat pack a square with
folded sides you put them all in
place and twist in shallow
screws you punch the pins
through holes fold back the legs
put in what you have mostly
piles of cut-outs from the papers
eight inches thick church
bulletins school magazines
Hansard Bibles a Students'
Union diary from his time
at Queen's reports things
he wrote hey presto got a DAD
BOX wrote that on the side not
sure why when we have guests
I turn it to the wall when
I want to see inside I make piles
on the spare room bed and on
the floor then forget what it
was I was looking for

the patient is pale
his skin cold and clammy
quick and irregular
shock can occur

send for a doctor
slow pulse and pallor
give him a sweet drink
lay his arms down

kneel at his head
place the palms down
your mouth over his
the first movement starts

breathing out breathing in
when breathing has stopped
allow lungs to empty
take your lips from his face

the patient should lie
in a cool, shady place
his head raised so blood
can drain from his brain

a   small   child   can   be   held

upside   down   and   thumped

an airy square a cube of plastic
poles a polyester sheet over
the top with windows on a roof
even flowers in boxes on the sills
a hole behind the painted door I
sat inside with her her second
name was bond I like the
thought of it the way it makes a
bed the b and d the headboard
and the footboard at the other
end the on contained inside we
played house tea poured into
cups not there whose handles
we held between thumb and
forefinger entertaining each
other as guests the grass was cool
we plucked the blades a handful
made confetti when the game
was weddings she became
a home economics teacher in
our house upon the lawn no
noise outside a bird sometimes
a helicopter

Family see jail chief shot dead

PM BACKS HER ULSTER TEAM

Tell us the truth, urges jail widow

THE HAUNTING OF THE NIO

Faith alive in Belfast **crosswords
on the back** moor days evade
iron prism

going   through   the   box   I   was
reading   Ireland   Johnston
Jones   Moreland   Morrison
McDonald   thinking   where's   my
name   McDowell   McFarlane
Nocher Orr it was the other side
she'd   cut   and   kept   the   headline
it was us

it's summer so the black bin bags
are stacked inside the car one
leans on the next one leans
on me our jeans inside our shoes
our coats our swimming
costumes drive along the
motorway so far it takes over an
hour our holiday it's two whole
weeks the Children's Special
Searchlight Mission mum
gets angry says I'm always
on my own when she's reversing
down the drive with me and all
the bags blocking her view
we act out Jonah on the beach or
in the church hall when it rains
hard shoulder birds are by my
window 50 pass with care

we go to New Horizons in
the big tent on the grass outside
the college made of concrete in
Coleraine all the wind gets in
through all the cracks where
the flaps don't meet the knots
undone on dirtied ropes

matches in small boats along the
coastal path a liner made of
plastic sweets inside until we eat
them light the match and watch
it glow inside the boat inside
your palm then throw it to the
sea and sprint down to the shore

we burned the boats we burned
the sweets we burned the
packages they came in burned
the leaves along the path we
burned the bits of paper dropped
on pavement slabs we burned the
sign that said wet paint burned
the grass and then the edges
of our shoes we burned our laces
at the ends the plastic melting as
they frayed we burned a tract left
on a bench we burned the
matches in the box then burned
the box the matches came in

a bullet is compelled to spin
due to spiral grooves unless
it impacts against some-
thing it will slow
down and
come to
rest

adhesive outline on the wall
where the black and white man
was he's face down on the tiles
will be until the clean-up comes

dad's sisters like the Twelfth I'd
never been where they pulled
the deckchairs off their hooks
the wall was darker where the
sunlight didn't go they undid
them where the pavement met
the main street so much noise
so many men their bodies
stuffed inside their clothes I
made each row disappear all
those shapes I put in place the
buttons of my Game Boy sticky
with orangeade a WHAM

Around noon, the girl took her
auntie by the hand to the rows
of rose bushes where her father
wasn't

Around noon, the men sent out
for fish and chips and as they sat
eating they watched the lunchtime
news to find out if they had
killed their target

Another murder book had diary bits to show the corpse alive alive-o here goes take the first step to a more secure future with the Northern Bank IN CASE OF ACCIDENT PLEASE INFORM Olivetti typewriters and adding machines 1968 Easter Day April 14 Come alive drink Pepsi the drink of your generation

next before Advent snowing hard
missed   church   got   tape
recorder history essay due I have
his books home from the Strand
I go there too still standing
from the thirties How historical
are history books? How effective
was the organisation of public
opinion for political murders
in the period 1714 - 1830 misread
purposes for murders his Ps have
no   descenders   Did   Becket
deserve his martyr's crown
a   quarter   moon   on
Hogmanay I see HEADSTONE
LANE NEW CROSS RIVER
UNDERGROUND

copy all this out
and I won't have to address you

shit

measure me in Beaufort scale
eight or nine approaching storm
Old Norse mad and frantic go
light-hearted   gaily   on

how did we spin the thread
that tethered each to each
me you you me how did we
exist before these letters all
these sounds I know sound we
had enough to sound out the line

between us

I had a sound for you by it I
called you daaaaaaaaaa deeeee
you had one for me the name you
gave me between one and two
syllables geeeaaaal you called me
your twice-voiced dawwww ter

diphthong name mine yours I
didn't know saw William inked
the caption on that yellowed
paper square with the photo
of our house and the sun
dial by the roses and nothing in
the drive stuck up on the kitchen
door said that was your name

mine was there and Beryl we're
still here the door was not a door
it was a frame with wobbly glass
made you look strange from
either side Blu Tack in all the
corners on the back these lists
the same name over and over
bold with little paras then
another and another orbituaries
she said the way we're moving
round the sun we say sunset but
it's wrong we learnt in school it
doesn't fall it's just we tilt

you're holding me she's holding
it the only one I have of me

and you we look to her we need
this three but soon we will be two

white   cotton   handkerchief
you   knotted   all   the   corners
& set it on my head under the sun
at   Helen's   Bay   I   know   it
happened in a photo I know it
happened from a photo I know it
happened and the photo is
something   you   have   left

                                        he left
the vertical went from | to —

a changing shape a fall a turn 90
degrees I look up vertical it turns
to vertex the apex the crown
of the head a whirlpool
swirling into avert turning
his head my mother shouting
BILL turning it towards what
was coming

on the carpet tiles the plastic
seat's a table for colouring in a
box of crayons said my name I
stay inside the lines a man inside
a lion's den a giant falls a small
boy hurled a stone it whizzed
through   air   in   dreams
a king saw seven cows all sleek
and fat and seven more bony and
thin who swallowed up the fat
ones ate them whole pink legs
white heads black lumps grass
green my sheets from Sunday
School The Good News we recite
the   old   ones   first   you   get
a bookmark and a lollipop for
every memory verse I put my
fingers on the Psalms and make
my own

                    shepherd

        let me rest
grass   quiet

                              go
        through the deep

            with me

                    my enemies   see
                              me

        know
                              my
        house

first I was an Eagle then a Juno
in Campaigners never made it to
the Inters girls and boys were
separate we wore green dresses
with a belt around the middle
and a beret when we marched we
marched in figure eights we did
badges called mum from a phone
box with 10p did a general
knowledge test they asked me
who's the queen I knew the
answer Margaret Thatcher made
cheese toasties for survival and
got a navy patch mum sewed it
on my shoulder all the girls
walked home their houses in a
row they shared a street their
front doors close their back yards
touched ours was big and all
alone

The Tremblies we call it when my
body shakes can't make it stop
except by sleep and I keep being
sick even when there's nothing
left it comes on me can't make it
stop we went to Doctor Breach
who listened to my chest and
asked about my movements I
said about my skateboard and
the way our street slopes down
you go quite fast the second half
and have to walk back to the top
cold medal on my chest I'm
breathing in and out next time
it happens mum gets out
a notebook writes down what we
had for tea I hope it isn't
Alphabites that I can't eat or
beans on the cover Zig and Zag

yew hedge a dense dark
evergreen she comes at you
sweeps the machine its cord
snakes round the garden as it
roars a skeleton its spine its teeth
razing new lines a nest a leaf
that which it finds it
eats a swordfish in her hands

blue with small pink flowers
white trim the shoulders
puffed you make it on
the Singer I was Susan

all these pattern pieces crinkle
on the floor when I walk on them
by the hearth I walk through the
wardrobe door on stage and onto
cotton wool the faun appears
for Lucy not for us behind
the curtain a box of cubes
Turkish Delight under white dust

apple tarts brandy
balls clove rock we had his Cash
& Carry card we walk the rows
stacked jars tower over our heads
black bullets bulls eyes on the
trolley with its wonky wheel
narrow headboards at each end
sea-sawing like a hospital bed

you hold the metal bars push
off coast across the concrete
polished like a magic lamp flying
saucers disco discs popping
candy lollipops psychedelic
rainbow drops below eyeline
snakes white mice skulls
double-headed worms
warehouse land with no daylight
where coconut mushrooms
sprout on coltsfoot rock and
toffee slabs the sherbet fountains
pop and giant dolphins swim
through liquorice pipes milk
bottles without tops and cola
held in cubes dummies gummy
bears midget gems love
hearts dew drops fruity tubes
I'm only small I've cherry lips
hard gums milk teeth
red chocolate hearts in our
mouths gold coins we pay and
leave

Hello it's me and I've just seen a
face in your guitar book corners
folded down your lyrics pencilled
in between those lonely nights I
have it now I hold its body
to my own and put my fingers
where yours were pressing
each string to the board I touch
each one & turn the key
until the sound I hope
is close

it's an Eko Echo made the sounds
she heard the sounds she heard
became her voice her voice
returned his words here come
to me to me he turned on her she
turned to stone her bones
hollowed a voice lives in her still

the second is First Song the last
Lunar Lullaby we are dust we are
spark we were light before dark

playing his records prepared
piano you said they obstruct the
strings to make it sound like
this put things in between Cage
did it first nuts and bolts the
fingers strike the keys the
hammers hit the 88 make
contact with what's strange one
man puts in ping pong balls
bottle caps takes his hands right
off the keys and stands the thing
vibrating still

I look for you I look so
many pages with your name
and images one man with
braided ponytails one holds
up two fingers with a Faith
& Freedom sign one is a king
his hand across his heart and
one's a baby with closed eyes
I try your shortened name and
others come there's one in
orange prison clothes one wears
a blue bow tie another's gauged
his lobe 10p in size one holds
the antlers of a deer and takes
an arrow from his chest two of
them are headstones one a
reverend one a soldier none of
them are you still I refresh the
page

as   a   small   boy   I   remember
question   marks   who   lived   in
that house

        a mistake could mean
    the death of an inmate
on guard

far   away   the   dog   has   lost
its blue ribbon

say the thing that isn't
                death

in   our   quest   for   knowledge
we   meet   the   unknown   birds
go past in summer

Statement of Witness

|
|
|
|
|
|
|
|

I did reside with my husband   Belfast

Maze

spells of duty

on 6 March 1984 at around 7.40am

breakfast

normal everyday practice

cloakroom

overcoat

hallway   pen, wallet and diary

hugged and kissed me and my daughter

we all left the house and went out

checking

checking

in the crouched position looking

I was down on my hands and knees

with a duster in my hand

strange things

unusual happenings

the car turned right

I shouted   a warning to my husband

both men commenced

I cannot describe

shots were fired they followed

shots being fired

my daughter

crying into the house

in my crouched position

I have no idea where

I could see bullet holes in my

husband's head   it crossed my mind

dying or dead

neighbours

hysterical state

the impression

woollen winter

first

                          lambswool

white

     soft

                               little impression

|
|
|
|
|
|
|
|
|
|
|
|

JUST TO SAY JUST TO SAY
JUST TO SAY a trio of cards
saying   nothing   to   say
just   this   just   grief   just
not what is just

                                                    a
figure

on a flannelboard he's felt his
arms reach out there's no one
on the green

a boy lies in the semi-dark
calling out to no one

        then dreams a father calling
him by name

here I am   you called me
here I am   you called me
here I am   you called me

```
here            I               am
you          called            me
here      I      am      you
called        me        here
I    am    you    called    me
```

Samuel dreams I dream of Ruth
her husband in her dreams not
dead but then the sun

change my name from sweet
to bitter

grieve and love another grieving

to live she loves her lover's
mother widowed too she keeps
her close a friend an almost
parent

where you go I will go –

they walked towards the harvest

have   I

                              strength

                                        if
                    deepest darkness
will   be

                              my cup to
the brim

baked potato alphabet laid out
on the sheet she lifted up and
tilted all the letters fell onto my
plate beside the beans I spelled
the words I knew and some I
didn't yet the T upended and a
bit lopped off you have an L
I make my name then take it by
the lip swivel it in place to show
her there I am in the news on in
the corner captions scroll from
right to left we watch to see
what's breaking

THE IMAGE came
pre-formed my colleague said
mother and child on all
the channels all that day

there's   the   shot
you've   hunkered   down
I   grip   the   bars

three-wheeling   thing
we   stay   like   this
in   the   exposure

an eminent Christian worker

                                        a bad man
impetuous at times
                            selected by the Administration
he instilled into them character and leadership
                                    to break opposition
devoted all his energy
                to the allocation of menial and degrading work
a man of high morals, honest, loyal, dedicated
                        organised and directed beatings in the jail
slayed   executed
                    murdered in the ordinary way
he appeared in silhouette
                    giving prisoners a hard time in Long Kesh
    a prison unique in all Europe

                        intolerable

                Government grossly unfair

            interference
                        not mentioned
                in the report

  Maze

        no Minister visited

                        blackout

                                years

                                                                lost

                their voices

                                on the empty air

H   not   O

HHHHHH

HHHHHH

HHHHHH

HHHHHH

not a tower

inside   with

cells   all   round   the   edge

blocks all on
the flat 25 in
each leg of
the H every
cell the same
only the curt-
ains   change

FROM PEACE TO PROSPERITY
the Maze Long Kesh story is
unique the Maze Long Kesh story
has been articulated in the
Corporation brand statement
From Conflict to Peace From
Peace to Prosperity a site once
associated with conflict Maze
Long Kesh has the potential to
become a transformational project
of international significance
the public interest in Maze Long
Kesh is undeniable since 2012
around 450,000 people have
passed through its gates for a
range of events and tours
development of the site is
currently subject to Ministerial
agreement on the way forward

THE VOID it runs for miles
another name for the inertia
watch to see it occupied
the sterile is where he will be
immobilised

															YOU SHALL NOT

have   the   body   it   has   been

||||||||||||||||||||||||||||||||||||||||
||||||||||||||||||||||||||||||||||||||||
suspended||||||||||||||||||||||||||||
||||||||||||||||||||||||||||||||||||||||
||||||||||||||||||||||||||||||||||||||||
|||||||||||||||||||||||the body in

the court||||||||||||||||||||||||||||||
||||||||||||||||||||||||||||||||||||||||
|||||||||||||||||||need not appear

																		a line of bars you

look   you   start

||||||||||||||||||||||||||||||||||||||||||
||||||||||||||||||||||||||||||||||||||||||
||||||||||||||| to see a face or chains

these marks align a lion's open

jaws||||||||||||||||||||||||||||||||||||||

for so long it was hard
to mourn thinking from that side
of things bad bastard screw
in the mechanism the
panopticon the architecture
of brutality knowing the theory
the cruel ingenious cage thinking
shit that's him on the wrong side
of the gaze

found a tiny silver sword not sure
what it's for

today I saw my

eye

drawn

out

a   ball   with   a   hole   to   let   light   in

                                    cast
me into the deep I am cast out of
thy sight in the midst of seas
floods compassed me about all
thy billows and thy waves
pass over me

in the belly in the beast
in the water black and cold
Jonah promising it all pleading
hear   me   save   me   now

I will look I will pay I will
sacrifice to thee

                    the beast released
its captive on the beach

BE PREPARED that's the Scout
motto prepare to meet thy Maker
that's another

a month before
he wrote a letter to All
in attendance subject My Demise

You will be gathered today
asking questions which only
a full investigation of the facts
will reveal

I am going to die
when it is time for me to die

that
chiasmus is a lie he was given
a gun a flak jacket and never
brought them home his face
blacked out he talked to the TV
camera in our front room it was
not time

I do not think

on the way down Commedagh
found a ram's skull picked clean
carried it home the teeth loose in
their sockets the bone like paper
dust left on the blade when a pile
is guillotined it sees through me
that emptied head

The Clouded Border I like best
it's like a cow on wings I saw one
by the lough shore where we ate
our picnic black and white in
patches ink spills on a tissue
that's another one The Tissue
Moth I've never seen except one
held on pins look at the
underside our teacher says our
fingers on the glass the
butterflies live under only they
don't live by The Speckled Wood
I spy The Gatekeeper
The Forester by them The Ghost
Moth and The Silver Y

the   carpet   underneath   our
seats   stuck   down   with   grey
duct tape you tear with teeth in
strips you'd think the rip of it
would sting your lips

                          three little
shelves   with   numbers   black
on   white   543   22   376
tot them up or read the secret
code

down from the Baptist Church
the big loud one with flags
and drums went there a while
they fell down on the floor
and spoke in tongues I learned
to too

best to start with k sounds
Kia-Ora like the juice key
ma me mi mo a jumble
that's the point it makes sense to
God   not   us   open
your mouth let out whatever
comes except in words you know
karala ratanda petuvu molongy

then the Spirit bends my knees
I hit the floor dream dreams
but slowly blood and fire in a
crumple and vapour of smoke I
stay moon into blood for
hours did my heart rejoice the
music plays my flesh shall rest as
flags wave known to me
the ways of life holy holy sings
the choir holy creaturely I
lay dead and buried looking up

mum says it's higher Katherine's
church I go with her when I stay
over there are angels in the walls
their eyes are closed lists of dead
men's names you stand and read
of one Being with the Father
through him all things were
made for us and our salvation a
Union Jack that smells like when
those little specks of dust settle
on the heater at the door enough
to form a clump then burn and
sizzle ropes clipped where you
must not go a marble floor like in
Flash ads white black white
all clean there was this part
where everyone turned round
shook hands mumbling pieces
afterwards goodbye we said
goodbye men in white dresses

o happy boughs o happy gloom
spirit culls **and** spirit-homes
shadows underneath the door
now I hear them ding-dong bell

MY   FATHER   REJOICES
that's what it means my name I
mean but did he

what if anything
was the source of his joy

was there joy between
us

before he left or after he walks
through the hall the squeaky
door saddle across the tiles
walking outside into the morning
into those bullets sailing through
the blue air into perforation into
a heap into gravel an almost
human shape into death into
silence   or   whatever

comes after

look to the mountains
       help
       will come

let
  your   awake

                 guard you

The sun will not hurt

          day   moon
          night

come and go

O Father
my father
my Father in Heaven
Father with his angels

my Father is always working
Yes, Father
No one knows the Father
No one goes to the Father

bury my father
only Father

My Father has given me all
things
every plant which my Father in
heaven did not plant

O Father
my father
my Father in Heaven
Father alone
         who remains in me

at it again you say we call it
playing the murder card when I
complain then get my way laying
down the dead father like the ace
of spades like a plastic poker chip
pushed across the baize like a
coin on the tongue to cross

this unlit root-erupted street this
night scene someone stepping
into view the sound it doesn't
make before the sound of its
release I'm going back I'm
learning lines for school what
wound did ever heal but by
degrees?

tungsten heavy
stone

the light inside those tubes

she stood there in the flickering

held his unworn clothes
and shoes

glowing white-hot
when the current passes through

filament   a thread

nothing   is   that   was   not
spun

they tied him up with strings
with ropes they wove his hair
into a loom then when he slept
they cut it off and shaved his
head she took his strength they
took his eyes they put him in the
prison mill to grind the grain
then made Samson a circus
clown a strong man temple
spectacle the hollows in his head
behind where eyes once were
the hollows throbbed blood
pumping at his temples one hand
rested on the pillar on the left
one on the right he bowed his
stubbled head clenched
his aching jaw and pushed

parallelogram the word
we learned in primary
four this sunlight on
a wooden floor

a   paler   shade
still grey that square the mark
there on the floor where DAD
BOX   isn't   some   sound
somewhere some sound along
the road in through the skylight
owls maybe no not owls round
here it's back in the spare
room again I had it here beside
my   desk   while   typing   I
don't   want   to   see   it   now

Safe　　　　　from　　　　　Save

preserve　　protect

a person
　a soul

　　a place
　　　　　　from damnation

　　　　　to offer salvation
redemption from sin to get out
of danger difficulty misfortune to
get away escape to keep this
document uninjured so what I
type survives the movements
of my fingers on the keys this
column on this sheet presents
itself as paper then becomes it
after Save as Template Save as
Save

the safe house on the street I see
through the window here beside
my   screen   I   must   have
known   that   was   the   street
but didn't know I knew until
I   started   going   through
the box

up at the Famine Village near
Five Finger Strand the villagers
are Topshop mannequins in
tweed bad wigs white shirts still
with their fold lines

after the eviction
scene the Irish wake and Orange
Hall a safe house secret passageways
to find and pass through
portals to another room and then
another opening o what a
funhouse boys and girls

the stuff of thrillers wigs washed
in the kitchen sink two pairs
of rubber gloves burnt in the
yard the briefcase tucked up in
the attic sub-machine gun snug
inside clean towels for everyone
the spinner going on third
time that afternoon

safe safe safe safe safe safe safe

the state

in which a gun

cannot be fired

at
a chest

or
a face

a container
for protecting provisions

refuge

doves cross flames sewn on
HOPE   LOVE   GRACE
in straightish caps on lamé
squares on bamboo canes we
watch   them   through
the   coloured   glass
eating our ice creams the
windscreen's got four bugs on it
you call them charismatics
waving those in worship Family
Viewing by our car we go inside
so we must be one and we borrow
Mary Poppins Herbie Goes
Bananas you put it in the slot
press PLAY the tape moves from
the left spool to the right we got
The Sound of Music from the TV
you record and then remove the
tab take that square away and
keep things forever watch it
watch it again but there's this
trick you stick sellotape on the
hole and everything can be
erased

there is a fountain filled with
blood we sit around the edge and
watch them disappear lift up
all the tiles turn on a tap and fill
it up with water takes all day the
people queue up to go down the
hole they step into the tank a
lady in a long gown weights
inside the hem to keep it down
our pastor in a white shirt wet to
his chest puts one hand on her
back one grips the closure
at her neck together they go
down under the surface
rise the organ starts from her
hair his their cheeks and eyes
streams of mercy never ceasing
call for songs of loudest praise

ice cream was the prize on
Thursday nights the lesson
lasted half an hour I walked
across a plastic tarp from the
doorstep to the swivel chair
protecting all the flowers
blooming underfoot I placed my
fingers on the blacks and whites
started what I'd memorised my
eyes locked on the bars I didn't
need

climb every mountain ford
every stream follow every
rainbow rainbow was the colour
of the strap on his guitar if
rainbow was a colour Noah saw
it from the boat the past the
plane he'd loved and left was
soaked and sinking deeper up
above his head the arc of every
colour Richard of York gave
battle in vain

you have changed

   your picture   you in your

daddy's arms reaching

out to   me possibly

my favourite

     I've added a comment

rivers of rain flowing   down

the Old Road I'm told

  it came across

     the main road like the sea

waves   water cascading

everywhere holding

          up

the traffic through Dundonald

new baby lambs

      rescued from

the fields brought into barns

to keep them from being

     frozen to death will

we ever feel the sun warm

our faces reading Enid Blyton
                    on the floor beside
your bed holding
                    up the book
so that you could
            see the pictures the sun
                        going
                down behind
        the Donegal headland

break   down   fibres
beat and blend with water plunge
the   deckle   in   lift   tilt   release
it   from   the   frame   and   press   the
page so water weeps from all four
sides it dries and you have paper
from the chains inside small cells

the   bloodied   dead   stripped
where they lay their uniforms in
piles   on   carts   bound   for   the
paper mill loaded six-foot high

first came clay
papyrus wax write on the skin
carve into shell take up the bones
                    inscribe a sign

what a paper trail this was what
does it all add up to lead to not
a   murder   book   and
not an archive not a fever not a
feeling all these things and none
it's what dislodges in my body
when I hear balloons pop pop the
birthday party I spent in the
corridor   outside   the   room
and   everything   inside   the
cake   the   streamers   party   bags
the tube of bubble-making stuff
a maze on its screw lid a little
silver   ball   making   its   way
through lines and lines you tilt
the thing help it along

                    the thing
scratched in the mind a stone
through glass

                moss in all the seams
the tarmac cracks kintsugi green

that first Christmas you stood in
the doorway as though to enter
this room with its fairy lights
and   tinselled   mirrors

was to forget that he is dead as
though to touch the artificial
limb of this tree you erected
with   cotton   wool   for   snow

as   your   child   opens
the gifts you have given and
wrapped was to ignore what
happened   just   beyond

the bay window to drop your eyes
to the holly and berries floating
in   water   and   glass   on
the   windowsill   and   not   look

through that window to the spot
you   see   in   your   dreams
where he lies holes in his head
and   chest   the   body   in

gravel
    blood broken windshield
                  glass

in our wood-panelled hall you
hold my dark hair in your hands
the ribbons from the tupperware
on the small shelf by the mirror
where he'd stand you move from
roots to ends untangling so
something could be tied you
know my kinks my parting line

the bobbles clink elastic on your
wrist drawn up over your hand
you take my hair into its circle
twist it to infinity that sideways
eight and thread it through
repeat until the band holds
fast and can be stretched
no   more

everything's   absorbed   even
puddles on the tar and droplets
on the feathers in the drive they
sit there going nowhere then are
gone where you're not looking

as   the   robin   sings   the
lunchtime news reports another
crash   a   bomb   scare   one
suspended sentence arrests our
ears now opened to the mower
we can't see beyond the privet
cutting lawns in rows in stripes
of green the tannoy-jangled ice
cream jingle going street to street

and damp dark cold the slaters
are   at   home   their   tiny   legs
carrying them back across the
greening grouting lining tiles to
what   lies   underneath   it   all
comes   up   and   out   and   in
the window to the bit without
the sun is open

NOTES

p.11: William McConnell's Queen's University Students' Union Diary, 1967-8.

p.20: Genesis 1 (The Good News Translation).

p.22; 117: Slaters are also called woodlice.

pp.24-5: William McConnell's Queen's University Students' Union Diary, 1967-8.

p.27: *Belfast Telegraph*, 6 March 1984; 27 January 1984. *The News Letter*, 12 March 1984; 9 March 1984. *Challenge: The Good News Paper*, August 1984. *Belfast Telegraph*, 9 March 1984.

p.28: *Belfast Telegraph*, 10 April 1984.

p.33: 'The Falling Bullet: Myths, Legends and Terminal Velocity', *Forensic Outreach*, 1 April 2013.

p.37: *Belfast Telegraph*, 29 April 1985.

p.38: William McConnell's Queen's University Students' Union Diary, 1967-8.

p.39: William McConnell's Queen's University Staff and Student Diary, 1968-9.

p.48: Psalm 23 (The Good News Translation).

p.54: *Pops of the 70s* (Hansen, 1970). *The Second Book of 50 Hit Songs by John Lennon & Paul McCartney* (Northern Songs Limited, 1967).

p.56: *The Songs of Ralph McTell* (Essex Music International Limited and Misty River Music Limited, 1976).

p.59: William McConnell, 'A Visit to Borstal', *Sullivan Upper School Magazine*, Summer 1967.

pp.60-4: Beryl McConnell, Statement of Witness.

pp.66-7: 1 Samuel 3 (The Good News Translation).

p.68: Ruth 1 (New International Version).

p.69: Psalm 23 (The Good News Translation).

p.73-4: Ref: William McConnell – Deceased.

Statement: Provisional IRA claim of responsibility, 6 March 1984.

Hansard: House of Lords Official Report, 15 March 1984.

Hansard: House of Commons Official Report, 9 February 1984.

p.75: Donovan Wylie, *Maze* (Steidl, 2009).

p.76: Maze Long Kesh Corporation, 2013. www.mazelongkesh.com

p.78: Internment Without Trial / Operation Demetrius, 1971.

p.80: Michel Foucault, *Discipline and Punish: The Birth of the Prison*, trans. Alan Sheridan (Pantheon, 1977).

pp.82-3: Jonah 2 (King James Version).

p.84: William McConnell, Letter of 3 February 1984, printed in newspapers.

p.89: Acts 2 (King James Version).

p.90: Nicene Creed, *The Book of Common Prayer*.

p.91: John Keats, 'Ode on a Grecian Urn'; 'Endymion'. William Shakespeare, *The Tempest*.

p.93: Psalm 121 (The Good News Translation).

p.94: The Bible (various).

p.95: William Shakespeare, *Othello*.

p.97: Judges 16.

p.100; 104: *The Oxford English Dictionary.*

p.106: William Cowper, 'Praise for the Fountain Opened'. Robert Robinson, 'Come, Thou Fount of Every Blessing'.

p.108: Oscar Hammerstein and Richard Rodgers, 'Climb Ev'ry Mountain'.

p.109-110: Email.

ACKNOWLEDGEMENTS

I am deeply grateful to Tom Chivers for understanding this book and working with dedication, passion and care to turn it into what you now hold. Thanks to Kate Wilkinson and Roisin Dunnett for everything they do to make Penned in the Margins a dynamic press and a good home for its authors.

I am grateful to the Arts Council of Northern Ireland for an Artist Career Enhancement Scheme Award which supported the development of this book and to Damian Smyth for his encouragement.

Thank you to Emily Berry for publishing five of these poems in the Spring 2021 issue of *The Poetry Review* and to the team that worked to print them.

I am grateful to Queen's University Belfast for the time to write afforded by sabbatical leave and to colleagues and students, particularly on the MA in Poetry, for talk about poems.

Thanks to Paul Maddern at The River Mill for desserts, a babbling stream and the chance to lay out and rearrange one hundred A4 sheets on the bedroom floor.

Thank you to my friends and family for your presence.

My first reader was Ciaran Carson. Ciaran, my debt knows no end. I miss our cortados.

My thanks to George Szirtes, who read and encouraged an early version of this book and gave me more language for what I was attempting. Vahni Capildeo's intellect and good company stimulated thought and growth. I'm particularly glad of a walk in the dark through the Newhaven wasteland at midnight. Conversations and rehearsals with Bob Scanlan have opened my understanding of the action of a poem, realised in performance.

Pádraig Ó Tuama's friendship and understanding of my poems are gifts. Thank you for loughshore days and for giving extraordinarily sensitive readings of this book in our public conversation for the Corrymeela podcast. Were it not for a conversation with my friend Tim Millen after midnight in his kitchen somewhere between lockdowns, this book would probably not be in your hands. Thank you for the prompts, walks and home-grown garlic, and for all the chat about paintings and poems.

Thank you, Jean.

Thank you, Mum – for going on; for giving me stories so we could. Thank you for making a loving future possible.

Beth Harding is my person. She knows all the ways I'm in her debt. Finding out that the person you love will support your work not only by doing five toddler bedtimes in a row but also by reading multiple versions of the thing and responding with insight and feeling to the poems – that was the great joy of making this book. Thank you, B.

And Finn, thank you for teaching me what language is and what it makes.